Raspberry Pi 3:

*Step By Step Guide From Beginner To
Advanced*

by
Leonard Eddison

Furthermore, the transmission, duplication or reproduction of any of the following work including specific information will be considered an illegal act irrespective of if it is done electronically or in print. This extends to creating a secondary or tertiary copy of the work or a recorded copy and is only allowed with express written consent from the Publisher. All additional right reserved.

The information in the following pages is broadly considered to be a truthful and accurate account of facts and as such any inattention, use or misuse of the information in question by the reader will render any resulting actions solely under their purview. There are no scenarios in which the publisher or the original author of this work can be in any fashion deemed liable for any hardship or damages that may befall them after undertaking information described herein.

Additionally, the information in the following pages is intended only for informational purposes and should thus be thought of as universal. As befitting its nature, it is presented without assurance regarding its prolonged validity or interim quality. Trademarks that are mentioned are done without written consent and can in no way be considered an endorsement from the trademark holder.

Table of Contents

Introduction

Congratulations on downloading **Raspberry Pi 3** and thank you for doing so.

The following chapters will discuss everything that you need to know about Raspberry Pi 3. You are not only going to learn what it is and how to install it, but also how to code with it.

There are plenty of books on this subject on the market, thanks again for choosing this one! Every effort was made to ensure it is full of as much useful information as possible, and please enjoy!

Chapter One: Raspberry Pi 3

Raspberry Pi 3 is the latest version of a series of single board computers that was first developed in the United Kingdom by the Raspberry Pi Foundation to promote the basics of computer science in schools as well as countries that are still growing.

When Raspberry Pi was first invented, it became a lot more popular than what the foundation originally anticipated. Because the program sold outside of what the original target market was, the accessories that came with the program were included in several bundles both officially and unofficially.

When asked, the Raspberry Pi foundation will say that over five million of their Pis have been sold before February of 2015 alone, which makes Raspberry Pi the top selling British computer out there. When November of 2016 came around, over eleven million units had been sold.

Raspberry Pi has gone through several generations since the program was first created and released to the public. The very first generation of the program was released in 2012 which was then followed by another model that was inexpensive and straightforward to use. Then two years later, another version came out that had a better design than the previous one. Each of the models is about the size of a credit card and were representing the standard mainline form factor.

With each new design, new capabilities that the previous version did not have before. In January of 2017, the newest model of Raspberry Pi 3 type b was released which typically goes for about thirty-five dollars. However, the new Raspberry Pi zero w was created in February of 2017 which was identical to the Raspberry Pi zero, but with this one, you now have the ability to connect to Wi-Fi and to use Bluetooth.

Each model of the Raspberry Pi comes with a system on a chip that also includes the CPU (central processing unit) as well as the GPU which is the graphics processing unit with a video core iv attached. Most of the CPUs are going to range from 700 MHz to 1.2 GHz with a memory of up to a single GB. The SD cards for the Raspberry devices are going to be inside of the operating system, and they are either going to be the standard size SD card or the micro ones.

Many of the boards that you can buy with Raspberry are going to have up to four slots that you can plug a USB into while also having an HDMI output and video output with a phone jack that you can use for audio.

The foundation makes sure that Raspbian is available for download on any operating system while Python and Scratch are the main programming languages that the Raspberry Pi will use. Because of how it is created, the firmware on the program is going to be closed, but you are going to have the ability to use an open source unofficially.

The concept of Raspberry Pi came around in the early years of 2006, and it is based on the microcontroller Atmel Atmega644. The schematics and layout can be found by anyone in public on the internet.

The trustee of the Raspberry foundation Mr. Eben Upton brought together a unique group of people who were enthusiastic about computers, academics, and several teachers that wanted to try and inspire children through the use of technology.

This machine was inspired by the computer that was created by Acorn in 1981. Each of the model names will indicate which of the models that you are working with based on the British educational Microcomputer that was also developed by Acorn computers. One of the very first prototypes came in a package that was no bigger than a memory stick.

There was a USB port on one end and an HDMI one on the other.

The goal of the foundation was to release two different versions that were between twenty-five and thirty-five dollars. However, orders for a higher priced model began to be accepted in 2012, and the lowest cost model was released in 2015, this model is known as the Raspberry Pi Zero, and it costs around five dollars.

Chapter Two: Downloading and Installing Raspberry Pi

You are not going to be able to run Raspberry Pi without first downloading the operating system.

You can find the software you need at
www.RaspberryPi.org.

Noobs

Noobs is a great program for Pi beginners. The word noobs stand for new out of the box software. If you want to, you can download a card that has noobs preinstalled on it from any retailer that sells Pi products. Or, you can go to the Raspberry Pi website and download it from there.

Noobs is easy to use operating system that has Raspbian installed on it in order for you to choose and download an operating system off the internet for your computer.

Noobs Lite is using the same installer but without downloading Raspbian. Everything is thing else is going to be the same.

Raspbian

We are going to go into more detail about Raspbian later on, but this is the official operating system that was created by the foundation and can be installed with NOOB, or you can install it on its own.

Most Raspbian is going to come with the software you need to be preinstalled so that you are able to do more educational programming than you would be able to on NOOBS. Raspbian is also going to come with several different programming languages installed with it.

There is a PIXEL image that lies inside of a ZIP file on the Raspbian operating system where all your features are going to be archived, but the old tools that were used to unzip these files are not going to be supported on all platforms.

In the event that your download for Raspbian is corrupted or is not opening correcting, you are going to want to attempt to use 7Zip or The Unarchiever before trying a reinstall.

Raspberry also supports third-party operating systems such as:

- Ubuntu Mate
- Snappy Ubuntu Core
- Windows 10 IOT Core
- OSMC
- Libreelec
- Pinet
- RISC OS
- And Weather Station

Chapter Three: Setting Up Raspberry Pi 3

Make sure that you have a mouse, keyboard, and a computer monitor or television that you can use for display.

Step one: slide your micro SD card into the SD card slot

Step two: connect you mouse, keyboard, and use an HDMI cord to connect to your display.

Step three: get a power adapter and plug it in.

There should be a red light to indicate that you have completed the setup process. Your operating system will need to be installed after you have set it up and you are going to use noobs for this process. You can install other operating systems if you would like, you do not have to download the ones that are available on the Pi website. However, you are going to have to flush your SD card and start a whole new set up for noobs.

You should notice that there are four raspberries at the top of your boot screen. It is going to show the cores for the processor that will now be set up and running as they should be.

If you want to, you can also light up your LEGS by using a breadboard as well as GPIO ports.

Chapter Four: Using Raspberry Pi 3

When you take a Raspberry board, you are going to be able to set it up and begin programming fairly quickly. You are going to set it up how we discussed previously. The Pi board can be used to create a number of projects, some of which will be talked about later in this book.

You are always going to need a connection to the internet and something to use as a display such as a monitor or television. You are also going to need a mouse, an SD card, and a keyboard.

You are always going be using some sort of code, so it is important to know what commands you will need and what they are going to do and how to use them properly.

There are multiple uses for the Raspberry Pi 3 board. Below are a few things for which you can use the Raspberry Pi board.

Home automation

Many developers are now using Raspberry Pi for home automation. Most of these programmers are taking Raspberry Pi and modifying it so that it is not only energy efficient but cost affordable to those who may not necessarily be able to afford it. The board is going to be able to monitor how much energy is consumed in the household in order to help the family make wiser choices in lowering their bill in the event that they are not able to afford their monthly bill. Thanks to the low cost of the Raspberry Pi board, this is one of the most popular solutions out there because most other solutions are going to be too expensive not only on a commercial level but a private level as well.

Industrial automation

A Polish company by the name of TECHBASE took the Raspberry Pi and became the first to design an industrial computer with it. This equipment is known as ModBerry due to the fact that it runs on the Raspberry Pi compute modules. There are numerous interfaces on this device. There are several serial ports and data can be inputted digitally or manually depending on what the need is. Through this design, Raspberry is no longer just on projects for homes or science, but it is being used to find solutions to a significant number of challenges that industries are facing every day.

Commercial products

The Next Thing Company created an OTTO digital camera that uses the same compute module that is being employed in Poland to automate their industries. Thanks to a kick starter campaign that was started in 2014, the entire project was crowd funded.

There are also other digital tools such as digital media players that use the module for making the device run.

The creators of the Raspberry Pi not only created it for being used on a personal level but for education as well. In 2012, there were questions brought forward to the board located in the United Kingdom in an effort for schools both public and private to get Raspberry Pi in their schools. It was the hope of the school that their school would have more an advantage with the Raspberry Pi in their school.

It was the Premier Farnell CEO that ultimately came forward and said that more schools were interested in the Raspberry Pi and this time it was not just the schools in the United Kingdom, this one was coming from a school that was located in the Middle East. They wanted each girl that was in their school to have a board in order to try and make it easier for these girls to get a job when they graduated school.

In 2014, the foundation decided that it was time to take those that were in their community and hire them so that they could make free learning resources available on their website for those that were wanting access to them. Some of the people that they hired were software developers and ex-teachers who were willing to work together on these resources. Under the creative commons law, the resources are freely licensed so that they are able to be shared with virtually anyone, and the Raspberry foundation encourages sharing these resources with those who need them on social media platforms such as GitHub.

A training course for teachers was also started know as the Picadamy where teachers were assisted in preparing and teaching a more technology-based curriculum through the use of Raspberry Pi in their classroom. It also aided in making sure that the teachers were constantly develoPing professionally through a free course that was run by the education team for the foundation.

It was not until 2017 that an MOOC course was launched working with the University of New South Wales where IoT (internet of things) would use Raspberry Pi online courses.

If you are interested in finding out more about how the Raspberry Foundation is working to further education as technology always changes, then you are free to go on their website and see some of their latest projects!

Chapter Five: Raspberry Pi 3 Basics

Before using Raspberry Pi, you are going to need to know the basics and knowing the basics means that you need to know what the device consists of before you go out and buy one or try and use one. In this section, we are going to learn the hardware and software basics of Raspberry Pi.

Hardware

The hardware for Raspberry Pi has evolved with each version that has come out. These versions have changed how much memory the device has and the peripheral device support.

Processor

Your Broadcom is going to BCM2837 for Raspberry Pi 3 which is going to have a sixty-four-bit quad core with 1.2 GHz. It also contains a 512 KB of shared L2 cache as well as an ARM Cortex A53 processor.

Performance

Raspberry Pi 3 has the quad core processor as we just mentioned which means that it is going to perform ten times faster than the first Raspberry did. This change came around because of the high dependency that there was for tasks that used threading or instruction set use. Most of the benchmarks are going to show you that the third Raspberry is going to be about eighty percent faster than the other Raspberry when it comes to parallelized tasks.

Overclocking

Most of the microprocessors that are used in Raspberry Pi are going to be overclocked at about eight hundred MHz while there are others that have been overclocked at a thousand.

Most of the new versions of Raspberry Pi contain firmware that is going to allow you to choose between about five different presets for overclocking when the device is in use so that you are able to maximize the performance of the SoC without shortening the lifespan of the board itself. The foundation did this by paying close attention to how hot the board became and how long it took for the CPU to load while always changing the clock speeds and the voltage that was put out by the core.

Whenever the CPU demand is weak, or the CPU is running hotter than it should, the performance is going to be slowed down and even stop due to the fact that the CPU is running too hot. When the CPU is running at its optimal temperature, then the chip is going to have an acceptable temperature as well which will in turn increase how fast the performance of the chip is. Depending on the clock speed, it can get up to 1 GHz depending on the board and where the turbo settings are.

Some of the highest presets are going to be around six hundred MHz, but it has been discovered the five hundred MHz can cause corruption to the SD card. Ideally, you are going to want the clock speed to be running somewhere around four hundred and fifty MHz so that you are not damaging the chip and you are not slowing down your CPU.

RAM

The Raspberry Pi 3 is going to run on a single gigabyte of RAM.

Networking

The newest version of Raspberry Pi is going to work with Wi-Fi so that you can connect without the wires. It is also going to have Bluetooth version 4.1 and will use a FullMAC chip that is not going to have any official support when it is in monitor mode. However, it is going to be implemented when you are using an unofficial patch for the firmware that it runs off of. And, if you are not able to get on the internet wirelessly, then you are going to have an ethernet port on the Raspberry 3 that will allow you to connect a ten out of one hundred cables.

Peripherals

All of the Pis are going to be able to have a keyboard and mouse plugged into them. They are not going to require any special equipment when you are using the peripherals. The Pi also has the ability to be used with a mini storage or MIDI converter which means that practically any device or component that has a USB cable on it, you are going to be able to plug into the Raspberry and use.

Video

Most of the video controllers that are on the Raspberry Pi are going to be able to emit what a standard television would emit when it is using HD or full HD as long as the monitor that you are using is able to support it. You can also get a resolution that would be emitted from a CRT TV.

The Pi 3 is not going to come with the proper decoding hardware for H. 265 due to the fact that the CPU is going to be more powerful. But, it is believed that the H. 265 is going to run fast enough that you will be able to decode any videos that may be using H. 265 software.

The graphics processor on the Pi 3 is going to be able to run at a four hundred MHz, therefore, giving you a higher quality of graphics than the previous Pis. The Pis are also going to be able to generate composite video signals as we mentioned earlier in the event that you are using a less expensive monitor with the most standard of connections which will usually be an RCA or a phone connector that is 3.5 millimeters.

Real-time

At the present moment, none of the Pis are going to be able to keep real-time because they are not built with a clock. There is a program that you are going to be able to get however that is going to work around this issue where the Pi is able to get the appropriate time from the network or the server that it is using to boot up which allows the Pi to know what time it is when it is being used.

If you want to provide a consistent time with your Pi for the systems, then you are not going to have to worry because the Pi will automatically save what time it is whenever you go to shut it down, the Pi is simply going to reinstall on the date of the boot.

Accessories

- Camera: back in 2013 the Raspberry Pi Foundation and their distributors were able to release the firmware update that would allow for a camera to be used with the Raspberry Pi. The camera is a flat cable that you are able to plug into the CSI connector. When you are looking at Raspbian, you are going to have to make sure that you enable the camera to run on the board through configuring the camera option. The Raspberry Pi camera is able to take up to a 1080p photo or shoot a 640 x 480p video. Three years later the 8 megaPixels was released to the public.

- Gertboard: the foundation made this accessory for educational purposes only so that the GPIO Pins were able to be expanded so that the interface could be controlled with a series of switches and sensors.

- Infrared camera: this camera was going to be part of the camera module that would not contain the infrared filter, and it is known as the Pi NoIR.

Software

Operating system

As mentioned earlier, you are going to want to try and stick to the Raspbian operating system which is an extension of Linux. There are other operating systems that you are able to use if you do not want to work with a Linux based operating system.

Driver APIs

The video core iv for the graphics processor is going to be using a binary blob which you will be able to prime into the graphics processing unit from an SD card and then only adding in the additional software when it has booted up. Most of the work that is done with the driver is going to be done with a closed source for the graphics processor and its related code. Any software use calls are going to run their code closed source, but there are specific applications that you can download in order to open the driver of origin that is inside of the kernel. The kernel's API is going to be designed for these closed libraries in order to make sure that it the Pi is processing correctly, and the code is not being messed with which could end up causing the Pi not to operate properly.

Firmware

All of the firmware that the Raspberry Pi uses is going to be closed sourced and use a binary blob that is freely redistributable. You are not going to find a lot of firmware that is going to be open source for the Pi.

Chapter Six: Installing Windows on a Raspberry Pi 3

Windows 10 released the operating system that would work on multiple single board computers. This opened it up to where it would work with Raspbian. But you can also put Windows 10 on your Pi board.

Step one: create an account with Microsoft connect

Step two: find the download for windows_iot_coreRPI3_build.zip file. This file is going to contain a file titled flash.ffu. This data needs to be kept in a place that you can access it later.

Step three: take a 8 GB Class 10 SD card and place it on your computer.

Step four: Open up your command prompt and enter this code:

Syntax

Diskpart

List disk

Exit

You will be able to locate the number for the drive that your SD card is connected to.

Step five: Microsoft has a set of instructions that you will need to follow in order to flash your SD card in Windows 10.

There is an administrator command prompt that you will use in order to place the image on your SD card by running this prompt. You are going to replace physical drive n with the drive number.

Syntax

Dism.exe / apply – image / imagefile : flash. Ffu

\ applydrive: \\ . \ physicaldriven / skipplatformcheck

Step six:

Take the SD card out and place it on your Pi board because Windows 10 is ready to boot up on your board.

Chapter Seven: Raspbian

Raspbian was created by the Raspberry Pi foundation as a Debian computer operating system that was to be used with Raspberry Pi. Mike Thompson and Peter Green were the ones who created Raspbian as a side project while they were working with the foundation. At first, the operating system was completed in June of 2012, but it is still constantly under active development so that the operating system can be changed and produce better results with each new version that is released. Raspbian is optimized so that it will work even with the CPUs that have a low performance.

Just like any other operating system, Raspbian is going to use a desktop environment known as PIXEL. PIXEL stands for Pi Improved Xwindows Environment Lightweight. Not only does it work on a desktop, but it is going to be able to be modified in order to work with an LXDE environment and can be stacked with the window manager known as Openbox so that an entirely new theme emerges.

Raspbian is sent out with a copy of the Mathematica program as well as the Raspberry version of Minecraft and Chromium. But, with Chromium, it is going to be a lightweight version so that it is able to be used with the Raspberry Pi system.

When you look at Raspbian it is going to do more than give you an operating system that is pure; it is also going to come with thirty-five thousand software bundles that are preinstalled and already formatted so that they can be installed onto your Pi without giving you any issue.

These preinstalled packages are meant to give you the best performance possible for your Pi, and they are always being updated so that you are constantly given the best optimization for your operating system.

The newest version of Raspbian was released March of 2017 and is version 4.4. This is an updated version of Debian Jessie.

Chapter Eight: Using Python with Your Raspberry Pi 3

Before you can get started using Python with Raspberry Pi you are going to need to gather some supplies in order to complete all of the steps that are required to do what you need to do with python.

- A micro USB cable
- A Raspberry board
- An Ethernet cable (this is going to give you a faster download speed than if you were to use the wi-fi)
- A microSD card that is 4 GB or bigger. You are going to want to try and stick to a class 10 card or better.
- A resin.io account
- A micro power supply that is 2A and uses a USB cord

You have to know how to use python with your board before you are able to build anything with your board. In the event that you are using resin.io and you are unsure of what to do next, there is a team of people who are going to be there to help you

Here are some of the moving parts of resin.io:

- Application: this is the devices that are going to run the same application code. Whenever a device is provisioned, it is going to be associated with the application. There is no limit to how many devices can be on the application. You also have the option of moving devices to different applications.
- Resin remote: this is the repository that is going to be tied to your application.when a code is pushed onto the master branch, a repo is going to be built and then deployed as a container to any device that is tied to

that application. SSH keys are going to be used to secure it, therefore, do not forget to set up the SSH key.

- Container: this container is used with docker.

-

SSH key

The SSH key is going to be used in securing the connection whenever code is sent to a program. To ensure the git connection, you are going to need to add the public SSH key. The private SSH key should never be shared with anyone.

All you are going to do is paste the public key into the UI box and make sure that you hit save. Or, you can import the key from Github.

Should you not have an SSH key, you should look at the documents provided by Github on how to generate the key pair for the operating system that you are working on.

After you have created the SSH key, it is going to be easy to use. You are not going to have to think about it at all. After you have set up the git push in your code, resin.io is going to take care of everything else.

You can also import the SSH key from Github by clicking on the Octocat icon. You are then going to be prompted to enter your username into the prompt that appears on your screen. you are going to need to set up and save your SSH key that you have imported before you go on to the next step.

Creating applications

In order to create a request, you are going to type the name at the prompt and choose which Raspberry Pi model it is from the menu before you hit the create button. You are going to now be taken to a new dashboard that is going to be specific to that application.

The dashboard is going to change as you continue to command and manage your fleet with Raspberry Pi 3.

Adding a device

On your dashboard, there is going to be a section that informs you of every device that is connected to your application. Not only that, but it is going to show their logs and their status.

You are going to need to click on the download resinOS in order to get that operating system. From here a list of versions that are available will be in your dropdown. The most recent version is going to be the one that you are going to want to use.

Warning: the versions that have the suffix .dev will be used for development purposes only which mean that they should not be used while in production.

Note: your .img is going to appear to be larger than it was before. However, your browser is going to download a compressed version of that photo and then decompress it so that the download goes by faster.

Before the downloading of this image starts, you are going to be asked how your device is currently hooked up to the internet that you are using. There are going to be two options that you are going to be able to choose from.

- Wifi: if you choose this option you are going to need to specify what your networks name is as well as a passphrase for the network that your device is connected to.
- Ethernet cable: there is not going to be any configuration for you if you use this as the default option.

After you have Picked how your device is connected, you are going to select the download device OS button so that you get the image for the resin.io operating system in order to configure it to your network as well as your application.

Once the download has finished, you are going to have a file with the suffix of .img and a name that is long with a bunch of numbers. There is a bit of text that says myfleet which is going to be the name of the application that you created.

Deploying code

After getting some of your devices connected, you are going to be able to implement the code so that you can start to use it to build your projects.

TyPically, the first project that you are going to do is a web server using flask which is going to serve as a static page.

You are going to need to put your code into your preferred git client. The repo is going to clone the project before changing the directory into a new directory and adding the resin git remote endpoint by running the command "get remote add" in the right-hand corner of your application page.

Note: on any other git client, you are going to have a different way to add the repository.

Since you now have your reference set up, you are going to add it to the application's remote repository. That way when you push any new changes, it is going to be comPiled and built into the server before being deployed to every device that is in that application's fleet.

So that you can deploy the code to all of your devices you are going to run this code:

$ git push resin master

In the event that you have to or want to replace the source code for your application with something new, you are going to need to force your push by running the code:

Git push resin master - - force

Note: when you perform your first push, git is going to ask if you want to add this to your list of allowed hosts, enter the word yes and continue with your coding.

Your code will be successfully comPiled and built whenever the unicorn appears in the terminal. This is going to mean that it has been saved to the program's image registry. The estimated time that this is going to take is about two minutes; any builds after this are going to be quicker due to build catching.

Now your application can be downloaded and carried out on all the devices connected to your application. You may have to wait up to six minutes for the first push to be completed. Your pushes that are done after this are going to go faster.

At this point in time, you will have a python web server that is running on the device and the logs are going to be seen on your dashboard. You can enable a public URL by going to the Actions page on the device settings from your dashboard. This URL is going to be able to be accessed anywhere in the world.

With Python being a coding program, there is not going to be much that you are not able to do. If you can code it with Python, then the chances are that you are going to be able to code it and use Raspberry Pi with it. You are just going to have to keep in mind that the Pi board is not going to do everything and you are going ot have to ensure that the prorams you are coding are going to go through the Pi program without any problem.

Desktop sense hat emulator

The sense hat emulator was designed to runo n the Raspberry Pi desktop rather than using a browser.

There are going to be sliders that you can use in order to change the values of your sensors.

You are going to want two versions so that you can

- Integrate the sense hat program with any Python module that is available or even with other Pi features like the camera module.
- To use it offline
- To accommodate the 256 MB modles of Pi that are not able to run the web version.

Your emulator is going to come pre installed on the Raspbian release however, you can also install it by using the terminal and entering this code.

Sudo apt- get update

Sudo apt- get install python – sense- emu python3 – sense – emu

Python- sense- emu- doc sense -emu-tools -y

Fromt here you are going to be able to access the emmulator from the desktop under the programming title.

This emulator is going to simulate the sense hat hardware that is attached to pi. You will be able to read the sensors or write the LED matrix that will be used in running multiple Python processes.

Your code needs to be written in IDLE like you have done before. In the event that you are wanting to port your code into a physical sense hat then you are going to need to change a bit of the coding.

This code

Sense_emu

Needs to be changed to

Sense_hat

At the very top of your program you are going to be able to reverse the porting to the emulator. But, this step is not going to be required in the web version of the emulator.

The emulator has a various number of preferences that are going to enable you to adjust the behavior of the emulator such as the sensor simulation that is also known as jitter. This is going to cost some of the time tha tis on the CPU and is also going to turn off the low end Raspberry Pis, however it will provide a realistic experience of the hardware sensors and how they are going to behave. You are going to behave. You are going to see the values that are being returned to you in your code according to the tolerance for errors of the physical sensors tha tyou are using on the sense hat.

The emulator is also going to allow the users of Raspberry Pi to participate in the Astro Pi competitions without the need to buy a sense hat which is ideal for the classroom when the sense hat may be beyond the school's current budget.

In case you are new to sense hat, you will copy and past a lot of the code that you see in the eduactional examples or you can look at other resources that are going to show you how to use the sense hat emulator.

The emulator can be installed on a Linux desktop such as Ubuntu if you are using that desktop.

Sense hat egg drop

There is a game from sense hat and Raspberry Pi that was created by a UK teacher where you can build the game and not only learn coding, but also learn science as well. In this game you are going be using the sensors for motion and humidity to determine how long it will take the egg to reach the ground and where it is going to land.

This is typically a science experiment that is done with high school kids to learn about mass and velocity. With Python and Raspberry Pi you are going to be able to do this but without the mess. On top of that, you are going to be able to look at other factors that are going to determine where the egg will land and how long it will take to reach the ground.

Chapter Nine: Tips and Tricks to Use with Rasberry Pi 3

Have you ever noticed that when you have some suggestions and tricks to use with the program that you are using, it makes it a lot easier to use that program? There are not too many things for which you cannot find tips and tricks to simplify use, and Raspberry Pi is no exception. Being that Raspberry is just like everything else, we are going to explore some of the tips and tricks that you can practice with Raspberry Pi in order to make it more enjoyable and easier for you to use.

Changing Your Keyboard Layout

When you first start using Raspbian, the keyboard that is automatically recognized is the Great Britain character set. However, if you want to change how your keyboard looks to something that may be more familiar to you such as the US keyboard, then you are going to have to get into the file that holds the configuration for the keyboard and edit it.

The first command that you need to execute is this one:

Sudo nano/ etc/ default/ keyboard

This is where your keyboard file is going to open up and will hold all of the code that has your keyboard set to the GB default setting. You are going to have to change the keyboard to the US keyboard that you want to use. You are going to see that your xblayout says GB and what you are going to do is go to this input and delete GB and input US.

There is no need for you to change anything else! All you are going to have to do is reboot your Pi so that the changes take effect and you have successfully changed your keyboard!

Changing the Default Local Time

It is always irritating when you are working on something that does not say the time that is right for where you are located. Raspbian is set to give you the UTC time zone automatically; however, you are going to be able to adjust it so that it represents your time zone instead.

First, enter the command
Sudo dpkg – reconfigure tzdata

Once this command has been executed, you are going to be able to Pick which time zone that you are residing in. After you have completed this action, you are going to reboot Raspberry Pi.

Whenever Raspberry Pi starts back up, you can use the command date to check the date and time to ensure that it is in the proper time zone. You should get the result of the day, the month, the date, the time, your time zone, and the year as your outcome.

Accessing your Pi with the name or the IP address

There are not very many people who know how to access a web page by using the IP address of the server that they are currently connected to. But, you are going to be able to as long as you add in the hostname of the computer that you are using to use Pi. In doing this, you are going to be able to use the name of the Pi device rather than the IP address.

Now, for this example, you are going to be accessing your Pi from a machine that is running off of Windows 7. There are obviously going to be subtle changes that you are going to have to change in order to make it work on a different operating system.

Make sure that you have administrative permissions on the computer that you are using or else you are not going to have the ability to edit the files that need to be modified.

First, you are going to browse your system for the driver's directory. This will be your host file, and it should have all of the drivers that your computer uses to run. What you will need to do is include the IP address for you Pi and the name that you assigned to it.

Whenever your local domain is reserved for SUDN (exclusive use domain name), then you are going to be seeing the domain name that has been utilized for the network usage inside of your machine. You are not going to be capable of configuring this like you will be able to set up the FQDN (fully qualified domain name), so your local names need to ensure that they are not conflicting with any external addresses that are located on your system.

So, at the bottom of your file, you should have the local host IP address as well as the IP address for your Pi. You should be able to type http://Pi.local into the browser now that you use and see the web page that is set up to be displayed on your Pi device automatically.

With the Linux system, your host file is going to be located in the /, etc. directory, and for those that are using Apple, you may need to go to the Bonjour service to find the host file that you need to edit.

Transferring files to and from your Pi

Whenever you are working with simple files on your Raspberry Pi, then you are going to have the ability to copy the code so that you can transfer the file to your Pi. Some people are going to say that it is not going to be easy to take this code and move it from the archive that you are working on to a different machine, but with the use of GUI, you are going to be able to accomplish your task without too much trouble.

You need to make sure that you are familiar with SSH file transfers or SFTP, you also need to have them on your computer where you can access them so that you can get the task down. SSH is going to be the secure shell. You can use an FTP without using an SSH but if that is the case you might as well just use the SFTP to ensure that everything stays secure.

The program FileZilla is going to be used to complete your transfer, and you are going to go to the FileZilla website in order to download it to your computer so that it can be used. This application is free of charge and opens sourced to ensure that you have access to all of the options that you are needing or wanting.

After the download is complete, there is going to be the proper software on your desktop; you should also download a zipped software, but try and avoid the installer due to the fact that the installer is going to give you software that you are not going to use necessarily.

Okay, now that you have everything installed, you are going to be on the main interface of the program. From here you are going to select the file that you want to transfer as well as the site manager that is located on the main menu so that a connection is established between the two computers.

A dialogue box should pop up that enables you to enter all of the details for the connection for your Raspberry Pi. You will need to click on the button that says "new site" and enter in all of the information below.

- The host box needs to have the IP address that is assigned to your Raspberry Pi board.

- The protocol needs to be changed to the SFTP SSH protocol.

- The logon type should be set to normal.

- Your login name needs to be entered into the user box

- Your password will then need to be placed into the password box.

- In the event that you want to rename your connection, you are going to be able to. This is recommended if you are working with multiple connections at once or to several different Raspberry Pi boards.

After you have completed this step, you will click on connect so that the connection is established. If this is the first time that you are doing this, then you are going to receive a warning box that is going to want to make sure that you are wanting to keep doing what it is that you are doing. Being that you are the host, you will want to click ok to continue with your process. If you are going to use this host for more connections in the future, then you will need to click the box that says you trust the host so that you do not have to approve of the host again in the future.

Your GUI is going to now be on your desktop, and the files for the Pi will be on the right side of the window. This is where you are going to have the capabilities to drag and drop files between your two computers so that you have access to what you need on the proper computer.

Editing files on the Pi with a desktop editor

Now that you can see the files that are on your Pi with the FileZilla program, you are going to go a step further and edit them on your desktop with your editor of choice. What you will do is log into the remote desktop session with your Pi and the desktop that is connected to it.

The first thing you are going to do is find a file in your Pi window that you want to edit and right click on that file. Here is where you will need to select the view and edit option. Should the file not have any program associated with it that will allow it to be modified, you are going to be able to find one on your desktop that you like to work with before hitting the okay button.

From there the file is going to be opened in your editor so that you can work on it until it is exactly how you want it to be. At the point that you have completed editing the file, ensure that you save it. Another dialog box is going to appear, and you will be asked if you want to update the file back to your Pi server. Make sure that you click on yes! This is done to make sure that you can edit the file and keep a local file on your desktop. Essentially, you are creating a backup file on both machines in the event that you need to edit the file again.

Turning the activity light on and off

Your Raspberry Pi board is going to have LEDs that tell you whenever you have power going through it and whenever the SD card is being accessed. You can find these lights at the end near your GPIO Pins. The first thing you need to do is execute this command. However, you cannot just use the sudo command; you are going to have to switch the root user as well.

Sudo -i

The I option is going to gather the root user's environment to ensure you are working on the right board in the event that you run multiple boards.

Your code is now going to show you which root user you are connected to so that you know that you are on the proper board. It is at this time that you are going to be able to turn the LED on or off by using a particular set of code.

To turn the LED on you will use this code:

Echo 1 >/ sys/ class/ leds/ led0/ brightness

To turn the LED off

Echo mmc0 > / sys/ class/ leds/ led0/ brightness

Once you have turned the LED on or off, you need to log out of the root user by click on exit or using the Ctrl plus d button.

Your /sys directory is going to work on the interface that is located between the user space and the kernel space. Since this is an implementation system file, the subdirectory is going to be pulled out of the kernel during runtime so that the devices that are running on the system are presented as a class.

You are going to see a highly complex hierarchy in your directory that is going to give you all of the classes and the links to those categories.

The class for your LEDs is going to be led0 or led1. While looking in the directory, you are going to have to find the trigger file so that you can see where the modules are in the kernel and which activity is going to be used to show the brightness of the LED.

Your LED is only going to work on two different levels of brightness, so essentially you are only able to turn the LED on and off which is going to be represented by a one or a zero. One is going to turn the LED on, and zero is going to turn the LED off.

Chapter Ten: Creating a Classic Game Emulator

With the Raspberry Pi 3 board, you are going to be working with a board that has incredible speed and is going to be different to work with than the Raspberry boards that came before it.

One of the things that the board offers you is the choice to turn it into a game emulator that is going to offer you the option to play some of your favorite classic games. And, who does not like to play the classics from time to time especially when you are trying to show your kids where their advanced video games came from?

Please note that unless you own a physical copy of the game, you are going to be creating a ROM illegally. Therefore, you are going to want to stick to the games that you own a physical copy of so that you are not putting yourself at risk of being caught and punished by the federal government. This can mean that you are fined or even sent to prison for having an illegal copy of the game.

Before you can begin, you are going to need to gather your equipment. Here is a list of the things that you are going to need to have in order to create your game emulator.

- A game controller with USB connectors
- A Raspberry Pi 3 Model B board
- The proper cables that will allow you to hook your board into the HDMI ports on the TV or monitor that you are going to be playing on.
- A case for your Raspberry board
- Keyboard and mouse that offers you a USB connection
- Micro SD card
- The HDMI cable that you are going to hook into your display device
- A power supply for the board

1. The primary thing that you are going to do is download the retro Pie project onto the hard drive of your computer. You will be able to obtain the download file on the retro Pie website.

2. At this point, you will need to download another image by the name of Win32DiskImager. After this has been downloaded, you will take the retro Pie file that is on your hard drive and move it to the SD card that you gathered when you were getting all of your equipment together. Before you write the image onto the SD card, you should ensure that you have the details correct so that you are not writing the image somewhere that it does not need to be.

3. Once you have the image printed onto the SD card, you will remove that SD card from your computer and put it into your Pi board. From here, you are also going to connect everything to the appropriate ports so that you do not have to do it later on.

4. Your PI should automatically boot up the retro Pie. After it has booted up, you are going to need to press F4 so that you get the command prompt opened on your screen.

5. After the command prompt has opened, you will enter the code: sudo rasPi config

6. The expanded file system needs to be selected before you hit accept.

7. Now back to your main screen, you will go to options and locate the SSH option under the advanced options. If it is not already authorized, you will need to enable it.

8. Moving on to overclock, you will choose medium unless you are playing games that have graphics that are more complex, in this case, you are going to Pick the higher option.

9. Just like always, you will finish with your options and then reboot your board.

10. After the restart is done, you are going to go to the main screen which is now going to be able to load your game emulators.

11. Your Pi board needs to be connected to your home network, and after you have ensured that it is connected, you will need to go to your network that is located in the windows explorer. There should be a table of devices that are attached to the network, and you will need to go to the one that is labeled RaspberryPi. You will need to double click it.

12. There is going to be a folder titled ROMS, and this is going to be the folder where all of your games are going to be stored as they pertain to the game emulator.

13. Your ROMS have to be unzipped before you are able to load them where they need to be loaded.

Please remember that if you do not have access to your Raspberry Pi because of the connection that it has to your internet, you can try one of these solutions.

- Take an empty USB drive and plug it into your Raspberry Pi 3 board.

- Wait until the light quits flashing before you pull the USB out of the port on your board and plug it into your machine.

- There should be an empty directory on the USB that is constructed just for the ROM files that you want to play.

- The ROM files that you have unzipped will need to be coPied and placed into their appropriate directories on your USB drive.

- Unplug the USB from your computer and plug it back into your Raspberry Pi.

- Once again, wait for the activity light to stop blinking so that you know all of the files have been reproduced over on your Raspberry Pi.

Congratulations! You can now play your classic games with your Raspberry Pi 3!

Chapter Eleven: Building a Streaming Program for Your Media with a Raspberry Pi 3 Board

This is going to be helpful when you find yourself owning an extensive collection of movies, music, and television shows that you have bought over the years. However, because you have so much, you most likely have forgotten what you own, and it is "collecting dust" on your hard drive.

You can set up a streaming program that is similar to Netflix and Pandora by using the Plex Media Server software that you are able to get for free!

To do this, you will be required to collect these Pieces of equipment:

- Your laptop your desktop depending on which one you want to work off of.
- Your Raspberry Pi 3 board

- A micro SD card

- A hard drive that is going to have enough power to support the streaming program that you are creating.

- A power supply for your Pi board. It is recommended that you use a 5V 2A power supply.

- HDMI cable to connect your Pi board to your laptop or desktop.

- A keyboard and mouse for the setup.

- You may also want to look into getting a heat sink for your chips due to the fact that using your board for multimedia consumption is going to cause them to get hot and potentially melt.

- An ethernet cable to access your home network if you are not working off of Wi-Fi.

1. To start , you are going to install the NOOBS operating system off of the foundation's website. You will need to go through an unzipPing process that is going to extract the files that you are going to need.

2. Place your SD card into your PC and format it so that it is using the Gnome Disk Utility.

3. Now you are going to need to change the directory that is on your SD card. You are going to do this by inserting this code into the command prompt. Cd / path_ of_ USB.

4. The NOOBS file needs to be unzipped on your SD card; this can be done by using this code: unzip PATH _ OF_ NOOBS

5. It is crucial that you make sure that the contents that are in your NOOBS folder are transferred to the root directory that is on your SD card.

6. At this point in time, you are going to need to plug your mouse, keyboard, and monitor into your Pi board while putting your SD card into the board as well. It is not a bad

idea for you to also connect the power supply to the board as well.

7. Your system should automatically start NOOBS so that you are able to install the operating system that you want to use. You will most likely want to install Raspbian.

8. After the installation is completed, you are going to need to reboot your Raspbian board so that it is now running on the new operating system. All of the files on your system are going to automatically be resized so that they are using the space that is open on the SD card.

9. Using your ethernet cable is going to give you the fastest speed during installation processes; however, you do not have to use it if you do not want to. But, you are going to need to get online with your new operating system and open the command prompt.

10. Enter this code at your command prompt so that you are able to find the IP address that is associated with your Raspberry Pi board. If config

11. After getting your IP address, you will reopen your terminal that is located on your laptop and change the SSH that is on your Pi.

12. By default the password for your Raspberry Pi board is going to be Raspberry; however, you can always change this if you want to.

13. Here is where you are going to need to update your system before your next install. It is always best for you to practice with a new distro when it comes to any software installations.

14. After you have updated your board, you will take the external hard drive and plug it into your Pi via one of the USB ports. Your hard drive needs to be formatted to ext4 in order to give you the best compatibility with the Linux system.

15. Now mount your hard drive and make an entry in the fstab so that the hard drive automatically mounts each time that you have to reboot.

16. At this point in time, you are going to install the Plex Media Server. Being that you are using a package that was created by a third party, you need to have their GPG key. For Plex Media, the GPG key is going to be: wget – o – https:// dev2day. De/ pms/ dev2day-pms. Gpg. Key sudo apt- key- add

17. Your repos also need to be included in the source file. Echo "deb https://dev2day. De/ pms/ jessie main" sudo tee / etc/ apt/ sources. List. d/ pms. List

18. Update your system again so that you are running off of the latest data that is available.

19. Plex Media Server can now be installed with this code. Sudo apt- get install – t jessie plexmediaserver – y

20. After it has installed, you are going to be able to run the service with this code: service plexmediaserver star

That is just the first part of building your own streaming program. At this point in time, you are going to now begin to set up your media server so that you can move your multimedia over to the Raspberry Pi board so that you can stream it without having it sit on your computer taking up space that you could be using for something else.

1. Setting Plex Media up is going to be a simple process, all you are going to be required to do is obey the instructions that appear on your screen. After it has been set up, you will be able to direct the service towards where your media files are in order to move them over. This can be done on any laptop or desktop that is working off of your network. All you are going to need to do is type the IP address of your Pi board into the web browser.

2. By transcribing the IP address into the browser, you are going to be opening the interface for Plex Media. Plex has a great feature that allows for it to gather information that is located on the internet

and taking your media files. But, you need to make sure that you have your media categorized appropriately or else Plex is not going to know that it is a file that it needs to grab. Therefore, you will want to create folders on your hard drive and place all of your multimedia in them. You may want to make folders with names such as "TV shows," "photos," "family videos," etc. Should you move a file into a folder where it does not belong, then Plex is not going to recognize them, and you are not going to be able to stream them.

3. Now, open the movie tab on your Plex interface and look at the folders that you are going to be allowed to browse. You should select the proper file that is on your hard drive so that they are moved into the new program. Do not rush the program because it is going to need time to scan and process all of the files that you put into it.

4. Not only are you going to be able to access your own multimedia files, but you will also be able to locate video channels online. To do this, you are going to go to the channels tab and install the channels that you are going to watch with Plex.

Awesome! You have now put all of your multimedia on Plex! But, how do you access Plex so that you can play that multimedia?

1. Open your browser on the network that you first started working with Plex on and put the IP number of your Raspberry Pi into the URL ribbon.

2. This is going to cause Plex to open automatically. All you are going to need to do is log into the media service and select what it is that you want to watch. Plex also can be modified from the interface that appears on your screen.

3. Before anything appears on your screen, you are going to be asked to set up the Plex

Media Player before plugging in the HDMI cable so that your Raspberry Pi is being displayed here you can see it.

4. To access the contents of Plex on a different network, you have the option of purchasing a PlexPass which will then enable you to stream the content of your Plex account on any apparatus that is connected to the internet. With this, you are also going to be able to share your Plex with your family members.

And there you have it! You have now created your own streaming program!

Chapter Twelve: A Personal Assistant made with Raspberry Pi 3

Personal assistants are going to come in handy when you are working on multiple projects and need an extra "brain" to help you remember what it is that you are supposed to be doing. The computer that is being coded to be your personal assistant is going to be smarter in some ways than a person is because a computer has more technology at its "fingertips" then a person may. Not to mention, you can talk to your pc and get the information you need without ever having to stop what you were doing.

In order to complete this project, you will need:

- A mouse and keyboard that will attach to your Raspberry Pi 3 board via a USB connector.

- An HDMI cable and a television that supports HDMI.

- A Raspberry Pi 3 board that already has Raspbian Wheezy installed on it.

- Extra wires.

- A Wi-Fi adapter with a USB connection.

- A double pole double is thrown relays that run off of five volts.

- A USB soundcard

- Part of a vero board

- A five-volt power supply

- A five-volt amplifier, you are going to want to keep this small so that it can be held close to your Pi board.

1. Update your Raspberry Pi board; you will need to connect your board to your network via an ethernet cable so that you are getting faster speeds than if you were just working off of a Wi-Fi connection.

2. After you have updated your board, you will need to shut it down so that the new updates are applied.

3. Before using the power back on to your board, you are going to need to connect your Wi-Fi adaptor.

4. Once booted up, go to the desktop and select the option that is going to allow you to configure your Wi-Fi settings. From here a new window is going to be opened.

5. Select the scan button so that another new window is opened.

6. In this window, you will go to the SSID and double click it.

7. A third window is going to be opened, and you are going to need to enter your password into the PSK box before clicking add.

8. Moving back to the first window that opened, you will be able to check the IP address and see that you are connected to your wireless network.

9. Shut your Pi board down once more.

After you have done that, you will be ready to set up the hardware that is associated with creating your personal assistant.

1. Open the plastic case for your sound card; you are going to desolder some of the connectors. You will need to solder where the connectors are so you are not harming the actual sound card components.

2. Taking your DPDT relais, you are going to make the push button on the intercom that you have gotten and connect the DPDT to that button. The second wire that is attached to the switch will need to go into the relay coil while the first wire goes to the ground. This way whenever the button is pushed, you are activating the coil and relay

switches. You can also add a diode in the opposite direction over your two Pins that are connected to the coil.

3. The Pins that are in the middle of your DPDT relays are going to have a positive and negative connection that is going to go to your speaker. The Pins that are usually open are going to be attached to the microphone's input for the soundcard. The Pins that are normally closed will be the output of the soundcard. However, you may find that the signal for your output is not going to be loud enough, this is why you need to have your amplifier.

4. Take the five-volt Pin for your amplifier and the five volt GND Pin and connect them so that you now have power flowing through your amplifier from the soundcard. You will need to connect the R+ to the R- to the Pins that are typically closed in your relay.

5. After you have done this, put everything into the intercom case and then connect your sound card to your Raspberry Pi board.

6. It is not recommended that you try to power everything from your board, that is why you may want to consider getting a three amp wall adapter. Depending on the wall adaptor that you get will depend on if you have to cut the connector to the adaptor and connect a USB connector so that you can power your board.

7. After you have cooked everything up, you will need to close the case for your intercom.

8. Take your sound card and configure it by opening your configuration file. You can do this by putting this code into your command prompt. Sudo nano/ etc/ mod probe. d/alsa- base . conf.

9. The part of your code that says: options snd- USB- audio index = -2 to where it says the same thing except your index is going to be 0.

10. Reboot your Pi board so that the new changes can be applied.

You are now at the point that you are going to be setting up the software that you need to run your voice commands.

1. It is recommended that you use the Steven Hickson voice command software that is going to allow you to have an easy setup and simple to use interface all while being reliable for whatever it is that you are using it for. The software can be located on his website and downloaded for you to use.

2. After you have installed the appropriate voice software, you will input this command. Voice command -s

3. It is with this command that you are going to be able to use the setup wizard and go through it to set up the voice command that is appropriate for your device.

4. After set up you need to enter the voice command -e so that your configure file will open and enable you to set up the commando's that you need and the actions that are related to it.

5. For configuration you will need to enter the script command = = action it is with this command that you are going to be able to set up the commands that you want your personal assistant to do. So, if you say play, then the program is going to know that you want it to play music. But, if you say something such as play game it will open up your chess game. You will be able to put in any command that you wish to be executed by your personal assistant.

6. After you have completed the editing process for your configuration file, you need to save it. Upon saving, everything is going to be ready for you to use.

7. In order to run the voice command software, you will enter the code voice command-c.

Your personal assistant is now ready to be used! Your personal assistant is going to be able to list to the commands that you give it and execute them appropriately. In the case that your command cannot be executed, then your personal assistant is going to take to the internet and find the answer that you are looking for. DesPite the fact that your personal assistant can now execute your voice commands, you are not quite done.

1. You are going to make it to where your voice command starts whenever you launch the program. In order to do this, you are going to go to your Raspberry Pi home directory and select the configuration directory.

2. Once in this directory, you are going to create a new list.

3. After it is created, you will need to access this directory.

4. A new file has to be created in the directory with this script. Sudo nano voice command. Desktop

5. Open the file you created and insert the code that is going to cause your voice command to start up whenever you execute the program.

[entry for desktop]

Type = application

Name = voicecommand

Exec = voice command – c

Startupnotify = false

6. Ensure your file has been saved before you reboot your Raspberry Pi 3, board.

Your personal assistant is going to be able to open up programs and gather information from the internet, however, there are going to be times that you want a specific type of information to be returned to you in a particular way. In order to do this, you are going to write out your own script using Python so that you can get this data from the internet and the data that you do not want is not going to even make its way to you due to the fact that it is not what you are looking for.

The biggest issue for this though is that your script is going to be written out and executed as text rather than speech, but there is going to be a script that is going to enable you to have your personal assistant talk to you.

1. The first step that you are going to need to go through is to get a text2speech.sh script. You can find this script online, or you can go to the blog of Oscar Liang and get his script that he has written out to convert text to speech.

2. The script that you choose is going to need to be put into your nano or text editor on your graphics desktop.

3. Just like any Piece of code that you put into your Raspberry Pi, you need to ensure that your script is saved and then made so that it is executable. You can do this with the following code.

Chmod +x text2speech .sh

4. By preparing this, you are going to be making the code usable for any applications that have the capability to convert text into speech.

5. The next step is to create the Python script that is going to work with the text to speech script that we have put into our program. For every script that you use, you are going to need to have a similar Python script. Your code is going to look something like this.

```
#!/ bin/ bash

Result = $( python the name of the python script you are using. Py)

./ text2speech. Sh $result
```

6. This script needs to be saved under any name that you want it to be saved under and then made executable as every bit of code needs to be made.

7. At this point in time, the code that you have written out can now go to your configuration file that you have for your voice command and then any text that is researched by your "personal assistant" is going to be spoken to you in the event that you have inserted the appropriate command.

That is it! Your personal assistant is complete and ready for you to use it.

Chapter thirteen: A Wireless Access Point

What you need

- Your Raspberry Pi
- An ethernet cable that will connect to the network you are using
- An SD boot card for you Raspberry Pi
- A device that is going to support access point and has a USB Wi-Fi port

How it will work

As mentioned earlier, you are going to be able to create a Wi-Fi Hotspot for those devices that need to have access to the internet but cannot plug directly into the internet; it is going to work much like an internet café does.

In simplified terms, you are going to be:

- Creating an access point to the Wi-Fi and broadcasting it on the channel of your choosing.

- Assigning an IP address to the devices that are going to use your access point to connect to the network.

- Joining the wireless and the wired networks together through the use of a Network Address Translation.

Step one:

1. Make sure that you possess all of the appropriate software installed. You are going to be able to find the software that you need online. You may find that it looks something similar to this.

Sudo aptitude install hostapd hostap- utils iw bridge- utils

2. Go into the file and edit the Hostapd part of the file. You are going to see something like this: sudo nano/ etc/ init.d/ hostapd

You are going to need to attach the DAEMON line so that you are able to create your access point. Your code for the DAEMON line will be this: DAEMON_ CONF = / etc/ hostapd/ hostapd. Conf

Now you are going to need to make sure you save your file and exit it so that you are not making any unnecessary changes.

3. This is the point where you are going to need to configure the hostapd.cof. you will be creating an open network or a WPA network that is secured. It is highly recommended that you create a secure network in order to make sure that no one is getting ahold of your access point and tampering with it thus allowing hackers to get into your devices and gather information that they should not have access to.

In order to do this, you are going to need to edit your file for the hostapd.cof so that the network that you create is secure. If this file is not automatically created when you download the software that you need, then you are going to need to create this file and ensure that you are adding these lines of code.

Sudo nano / etc/ hostapd/ hostapd.cof

Ctrl_ interface = / var/ run/ hostapd

This is going to be the basic configuration for your access point.

Macaddr _ acl = 0 autho_ algs =1

Many of your more up to date wireless drivers are going to have the kernel driver.

For your local configuration, you will use this code

Interface = wlan0

Bridge = br0

Hw_mode = g

Ieee80211n=1

Channel = 1

Ssid = raspberry pi _ ap

Macaddr_ acl = 0

Autho_algs = 1

Ignore _ broadcast _ ssid = 0

Wpa = 3

Wpa _ passphrase = MY_ PASSPHRASE
Wpa_ key_ mgmt. = WPA- PSK

Wpa_ pairwise = TKIP

Rsn _ pairwise = CCMP

Ensure that you are saving and closing your file when you are done adding in the code that needs to be added!

It is also essential to know that you need to change the ssid, the channel, and the passphrase to things that only you are going to know and the people who are accessing your internet will know. The ssid is typically going to be the name of the hotspot that you have created that other devices are going to see. The passphrase is going to be the password that you are using to ensure that your network is secure from hackers and those that would want to get into your internet and gather your personal information.

Chapter fourteen: Command Glossary

These commands are going to be able to be used with your Raspberry Pi to accomplish goals that you want with your Raspberry Pi board.

Apt- get

This code has two different parts. The first part is going to be for advanced packaging tool which tells the program which software packages it needs to manage, and these packages are already going to be installed on your Linux machine, it is going to work best with the Debian Linux machines. And since Raspbian is Debian, then you are going to be allowed to use apt- get.

The apt is going to be a process that will simplify how you manage the software that is on the UNIX computer system all by automating the retrieval, installation, and configuration of the software packages that are already on your Raspberry Pi board.

When this code first came out, it was known as "dependency hell" due to the fact that some of the packages that were being installed had to go through a manual installation process. It caused the user not to know what they were doing, thus causing them to make a mistake and not get everything installed as it was supposed to be.

Apt – get is commonly used with Raspberry Pi when you use the prefix sudo so that you have the proper permission.

When you want to renew your local files to ensure that they contain the newest packages that have changed, you will use apt- get update.

Apt- get upgrade is going to place the latest versions of the packages in your system if they are already installed and a new version is readily available to be put on your computer. If there are new releases that cannot be upgraded without additional steps, they are going to be left as they are so that you have to upgrade them on your own.

You will need to do the update code before you do the upgrade code so that you can see if any packages are in need of being updated.

Apt – get install

With this code, you are going to be able to install or upgrade the packages that are in need to be updated or installed onto your Raspberry Pi. This includes any packages that are dependent.

Cat

Your cat command is going to do multiple things. First off, the word cat stands for catenate which is going to connect multiple things in a series. This will be one of the most common uses that you are going to use cat for. You can also use cat for things like

- Joining a text file to another text file
- Showing text files in your command line
- Copying the text file into a new document.

Let us imagine that you are wanting to show a text file on the screen that you are working with, you are going to use cat and the file name.

Once this command has been executed, you are going to see the file on the screen. However, if your file is a large file, then some of the contents are going to be dumped so that they result in a scrolling waterfall of text on the screen just to ensure that everything is placed on the screen for you to see.

You also have the option of displaying two different files one right after the other with the cat command. You will use the same command that you used earlier, but you are going to add in the word bar so that they appear on your screen one after the other.

You do not necessarily have to have a file sent to your screen, you can also have that file forwarded to a different file, or we can rename that file with the cat command. You are going to use the same cat command that you have been using except now you are going to add in newfile.txt so that a new file is created from the file that you have selected.

This is essentially the same process as copy the file and redirecting it. However, if you want to take it a step further, you have the option of taking that file and combining it with the original file. So, your code is going to look something like this.

Cat file name. Txt bar. Txt > new file. Txt

Lastly, you have the option to use cat to append a file that already exists. In orde to do that, your code will look a little something like this.

Cat file name. Txt >> file that already exists. txt

The double arrow is going to redirect your operator so that it searches for the other file that you already have on your system to add the new file to it.

Please remember where it says file name, you are going to need to put the name of the file that you want to work. If you brought in a file name, you are going to receive and error message because the system is not going to know what file you want to work.

Conclusion

Thank you for making it through to the end of *Raspberry Pi 3*, let's hope it was informative and able to provide you with all of the tools you need to achieve your goals whatever it may be.

The next step is to use the information that you have learned in this book and get to coding with Raspberry Pi 3. You are going to be able to create a lot of projects that are going to improve your life so that it is easier.

Raspberry Pi 3 has a lot of potential to change the world; the proper people are going to have to be able to code with it. Therefore this book is meant to reach out to those that want to learn how to code with the board and use it.

Finally, if you found this book useful in any way, a review on Amazon is always appreciated!

Thank you and good luck.

Python

A Complete Step-by-Step Guide to Programming with Python

Leonard Eddison

The legality extends to creating a secondary or tertiary copy of the work or a recorded copy and is only allowed with express written consent of the Publisher. All additional rights are reserved.

The information in the following pages is broadly considered to be a truthful and accurate account of facts, and as such any inattention, use or misuse of the information in question by the reader will render any resulting actions solely under their purview. There are no scenarios in which the publisher or the original author of this work can be in any fashion deemed liable for any hardship or damages that may befall them after undertaking information described herein.

Additionally, the information found on the following pages is intended for informational purposes only and should thus be considered, universal. As befitting its nature, the information presented is without assurance regarding its continued validity or interim quality. Trademarks that mentioned are done without written consent and can in no way be considered an endorsement from the trademark holder.

Table of Contents

Introduction

Congratulations on downloading your personal copy of *Python: A Complete Step-by-Step Beginners Guide to Programming with Python.* Thank you for doing so.

The following chapters will discuss the way that you can learn Python and how the programming language can help you to have a more enjoyable experience while you are programming.

You will discover how important it is to make sure that you are using the program in the right way and that you are going to truly get the most out of it based on what you learn in the book.

The final chapter will explore the ways that you can apply Python programming language to various other aspects of your programming career and also how you can make it a career. Knowing Python is great if you want to create different things on your own, but knowing how to use Python in a career sense is a great way to ensure that you can enjoy profits that come from the programming language.

Imagine having financial freedom just from being able to use a programming language for yourself and others! There are plenty of books on this subject on the market. Thanks again for choosing this one! Every effort was made to ensure it is full of as much useful information as possible. Please enjoy!

Chapter 1:

Getting Your Program Set Up

You will need to make sure that you are going to be able to use Python to create programs. The thing about that is, though, that you need to have a good environment for those programs.

The first thing that you will need to do is install Python. There is a very small chance that the program is already installed on your machine, but if it is not, it is very simple to install yourself.

If you are using Windows, you will just need to search for Python. You will need to use a command line on Mac and Linux if you want to be able to find Python on either of those systems. Once you have found it, you can skip ahead and get started using it.

If you did not find Python on your computer, you will need to download it.

Start out by going to python.org so that you can find the program. There is a section on the website that is labeled "downloads," and you just need to click on it. There, you will see the latest version of Python.

There will be a download button that is close to it. Make sure that it is the real download button, though, because there might be ads for other things that are close, so be sure that you are actually clicking the right button.

You will have to go through the install wizard that was created by Python, but as soon as that is complete, you are good to go.

You will also need a text editor that converts to plain text. Microsoft has this kind of system, or you can choose to download any plain text program of your choice.

See, that wasn't so hard, was it? Python is actually very simple to understand, and you will see that each of the steps are easy to follow if you just take your time and do them in the right order.

Chapter 2:

The Math Aspect of Python

You will need to create files as you go throughout this book. It will not only help you to keep track of what you are doing, but it will also help you practice all of the things that you can do while you are learning Python. It is a great way for you to learn, and it will give you the chance to truly make the choices that you need for your Python experience. The first file that you should create is ch2.py. This is something that you will need to do each chapter up until we get to Chapter 11 where you will learn exactly how to apply the skills you have learned throughout the first 10 chapters of the book.

The first thing that you will learn about during this time includes variables and values.

V&V

Variables come first and have a given value. They are used in nearly every type of programming language, and they are able to see the way that things are done. Here is an example of what it would look like in Python:

car = "Volkswagen Jetta"

You don't need to use the string term like you would use in other types of language. There are different types that you can use with python. Make sure, though, if you want to use a string, you use the "" around the item that you are putting in a string. Otherwise, Python will just recognize it as a basic idea.

Here are some definitions of the different types of variables that you will find in Python:

Integer – 6

Float – 6.41

Boolean – True (or False)

String – Feta

Now, you are going to practice it.

In the file that you created, you're going to verify the integers and the strings that are included with the different types of variables. Use your favorite food and a set number of days. You can choose to use these examples or, if you feel daring, you can use your own.

favoriteFood = "hot pocket"

days = "30"

After that, you can give it a command which is so easy to do.

print "I love to eat %s." %favoriteFood.

The variables, if you hadn't figured it out, are the ones on the left side, and the values are the ones on the right that determine what the variables are going to do.

Operator

There are other ways that you can add additional information. For example, you can change your favorite food to your second favorite food:

```
favoriteFood = "hot pocket"
days = "30"
print "I love to eat %s." %favoriteFood.
favoriteFood = "avocado"
```

That isn't the end of it though. You can make a new print statement that will be added to the string.

```
print "Actually, I have had %d days in a row. I need to move on to something else. My new favorite food is %s." %days, favoriteFood).
```

Now that this second part is included with the string, it should make more sense for you to try and get the total favorite food amount included in the sentence. This is how you put things together with the Python language. When you do this, it will show up in different ways, and it will allow you to try new things with it.

If you have variables that you want to be able to use, the best way to do it is to start out with basics ones like the ones that were listed above. They are simple, are easy to expand on, and will give you the chance to be able to try new things with the Python codes that you have chosen to use. It can sometimes be complicated to figure out which codes are going to work best for you, so keep that in mind before you work on the different aspects of Python.

Once you have all of those codes done, you can add in new variables. They are all written the same way, just make sure that you use the values that you want for each of the variables.

Essentially, you would be able to tell a story the whole way through based on the variables and the values that you have. The best part is, though, that it will change based on what you use and the context that you use it in. For example, you could use it for a webpage that gives the things that you have recently read. When you read the first book that you are enjoying, you can put that into the information. After that, you can try different avenues that will allow you the chance to put new information into it.

The variable–value outlook is one that is great for trying with websites that have different listings, that have variables that will constantly change, and that has information in it that you will need to keep people updated on.

If you want to change things within the variables, make sure that you always put a new command in the line that you want it to change. Without the command, you won't be able to show people what you are talking about, and it will not appear on the programming that you have worked so hard to be able to create. Essentially, it will be null of doing any good for you or for the way that you want to try new things with the variables that you have. It can be difficult to understand and to do, but it will be a great way for you to get started with your programming.

As you learn more about commands, you can try new things. You don't always have to use the print command, but it is one that is simple to use and also simple for you to understand. It is what most people start with in programming, and it is easy to use no matter what level of programmer you are or how much experience you have with Python.

Now, you will learn how to compare the values that you have.

Chapter 3:

Statements for Conditions

There are many things that you can do with values and variables, but the ability to compare the ability to compare them is something that will make it much easier for you to try and use Python. It is something that people will be able to do no matter what type of values that they have, and they can make sure that they are doing it in the right way so that their program will appear to be as smooth-running as possible.

To compare your variables is one of the many options that Python offers you, and the best way to do it is through an "if statement."

Now, you will create your Chapter 3 file by saving it as ch3.py. This is what you will need to be able to do.

Here is the way that an incidental will look:

apples=6

bus = "yellow"

```
if apples == 0:
print "Where are the apples?"
print "Did you know that busses are %s?" bus
```

Run the code through your python program. It will look like this.

Did you know that busses are yellow?

The easiest way to understand why the output looked like this is because the apples were not included with the variation. There were not zero apples, and that was something that created a problem with the code. For that reason, it wasn't put in the output because there was no way to do it and no way to make it look again.

To make sure that you are going to be able to use it with a not statement, you can use another if statement in combination with that not.

```
if not apples == 0
print "How 'bout them apples!"
```

Now, you can try to run the code again through the program that you created.

It will look like this:

How 'bout them apples!

Did you know that busses are yellow?

Both of the things that you wrote in the code are included with the statements, and then, you will be able

PITHON

to try different things. If you do not want to write out the not statement, you can simply use the "!"

if apples! = 0

print "How 'bout them apples!"

This will help you to put the code in and will make it easier for you to be able to write out in the code that you are creating. It can sometimes be hard to figure out the right way to do it and then you will be able to apply it.

When there is an input in your program, such as the number of apples that someone wants or a fact that they have that they can teach you about, the output will look the same. Either they will get a statement about the apples, or they will get a statement about the bus being yellow. If there are no apples that are put into the equation, then you will have the output show up as "Where are the apples"

The conditionals that you use are made up of simple expressions. When you break them down into even smaller pieces, it is easy to understand how they can be used and what you will be able to do with the expressions that you have in the things that you do. It will also give you the chance to be able to show that there is so much more than what you initially had with the variables and values.

Absolutes

There is a way to create the conditionals so that there is a block of codes that will show you whether or not there is a conditional, and it has something that it can do even if the conditional is not true and cannot be verified with the different things that you do.

That is where the absolute conditionals come into play. You will need to see whether or not there are different things that you can put in.

Create the variable

apples =

Now, you will need to put the input in with the different things that you have created in Chapter 2 version of the file that you saved.

print "What is your age?"

age = raw_input()

That is the way that you will be able to see how old someone is. But, how exactly does that relate to the number of apples you have?

It doesn't, it just shows you how the variable works so that people can put things in.

You'll create

apples = raw_input ("What number of apples are there?/n")

That is the easiest part of it and will help you to create the variable that you need for the rest of it.

if apples == 1:

print "I don't know what to do with just one apple!"

You'll get an error though because apples is actually just a string and you need to make it an integer.

Simple:

int(string)

Now it will look like this:

apples = raw_input("What number of apples are there?/n")

apples = int(apples)

if apples == 1

print "I don't know what to do with just one apple!"

Put this whole string into your file or change the wording around a bit so that you can figure out what you want to do with it (that is truly great practice for you). When you have put it in, run it through.

The code will work because you created a variable, you added different elements to it, and you allowed for the input of the "apples" in the sequence so that you would be able to show how things worked with it.

This was one of the greatest ways that you could do new things, and it also allowed you the chance to be able to try new things so that you were doing more with it.

While you are creating strings of integers, you will need to make sure that you are transforming them into integers instead of simple strings so that you can make sure that they show up and there are no error codes.

This is your first program. You don't want to show tons of errors, do you?

Chapter 4:

Formats for Strings

Now that you have learned to create the variables and what you can do with the variables, it is important to look at the way that you can format the strings so that they will do exactly what you want. This is where the print commands come in and the different things that you will be able to do with them. If you do not want to do the print command, you can figure out different ones that work for you and what they will be able to do. In this chapter, you'll be creating a new file and changing the way that you can do different things with the strings that you have created. By formatting them to do exactly what you want, you will be well on your way toward being a very independent programmer.

When you break it down, the print command that you were doing was nothing more than a format statement that shows the way that things will appear on the program.

Create your ch4.py file so that you can use it in combination with the other strings that you have created in the previous chapters.

ferrets = 3

chickens = 4

llamas = 0

bison = 1

goats = 3

Then, create it so that it shows up in the print style sequence that you wanted to be able to use for your output.

print "I bought %d ferrets, and I also purchased %d chickens." % (ferrets, chickens)

print "I bought %d llamas /n%d bison, / nand %d goats" % (llamas, bison, goats)

print "The total I bought in allows me to have :/n/t%d livestock." % (llamas + bison + goats)

Run this through your Python program so that you can try something new and see what it is able to do to make it look better for you.

I bought 3 ferrets and I also purchased 4 chickens. I bought 0 llamas, 1 bison, and 3 goats. The total I bought in allows me to have 4 livestock. This is the easiest way to write it, and that is why we will continue to use the print format so that you can make sure that it shows up. It is a very simple process and one that you will be able to make the most use out of depending on the information that you want to put into it.

To be able to create the string to print out, you will need to make sure that there are things that you can print. These are the integers that you will be able to use no matter what type of string that you wanted. This is something that will make your printing better and will allow you to see that there are different things that can be printed

(Hopefully, by now, you realize that "printing" does not actually refer to sending information to a physical printer like the way that you would normally think of printing. Instead, it simply "prints" the words into the program that you have so that you will be able to see the different aspects of each of the things that you are doing. Without the printing, it will not show up on your program.)

Escape Sequences

The / marks that are used throughout the formats, and the sequences are used for escaping from the code. It is as simple as writing one when you want the program to stop using the code and, instead, focus on the text that you are going to be able to use.

With the escape sequence, you should make sure that you are only using them in the way that you want to stop coding. If you try to use them in the middle of the code, it will ruin the whole thing, you will need to go back and rewrite it all, and it can be very difficult to try and get the exact thing done the way that you had written in the past. When you are working with the codes that you have, you will want to use an escape code if you are not using a statement.

For example, use the escape code that you want to show people that you want to stop using the codes. Simple do something like "I have" or "There are." These are the simplest statements that you can use. After you write those, put the code in and then put / into the end of the code so that it will stop coding it, and you can actually try new things with the information that you are putting into your program.

As you learn more about the different codes and the ways that they are able to work within the Python code, you will be able to try new things. It is always important to remember to escape when you no longer want to write the codes out and when you want to be able to try new things. It is imperative to the way that you change your codes that you do this and that you make sure that you are doing it all of the time that you are trying new things. Without the ability to make the codes that you want, you will struggle with programming.

The next chapter is very complicated. It has data sets that are difficult to understand, and you will need to make sure that you are prepared by writing out simple codes. If you did not "get" something in one of the previous chapters, go back to review it. It is also a good idea to try something new and put the practices that were outlined in those chapters to good use. If you haven't done so already, try to make sure that you are using the codes in the right way and that they are put into the different parts of your files.

When you are comfortable with the concepts outlined in Chapters 2–4, you will be alright to move onto Chapter 5. If you are struggling, always go back to review what you did.

Chapter 5:

Using Data Sets

Now that you have learned the true basics of Python and what you can do with it, you'll need to start working with data sets. This is one of the only ways that you will be able to truly get the most out of Python and create a program that really works for you with the different things that you want to do.

If you thought that it was simple up until this point, don't worry, it will still be simple. You'll just have to make sure that you follow each of the steps and pay attention to how important it is to learn the different types of steps before you get started.

Lists

The lists that you are going to create are just like the strings that you created in the earlier chapters, but they will be able to do more for you than what the strings were able to do on their own. Lists look something like this:

int grades (4) = {32, 58, 12, 100}

This are the way that you can create different things. You could also write it out as integers with the student numbers, but that would take a really long time and you might not be able to get what you wanted out of the sets that you are doing. For that reason, you can put them together into a set of data (a data set, get it, it's simple).

You'll need to change the grade so that there is a new one in the array that you have and so that you can make sure that you will be able to try more with what you have. It is very easy to try new things and to make sure that you are going to be able to get the sets that you need when you want to add more to the information.

Arrays are the same as lists except they specify the number of things that they can hold in them. Lists seem to work better because of the following reasons:

- They can have their size adjusted the right way.
- You don't need to have just one in a set of data.

This is great for later on when you start to learn about children and offshoots that come from the data you put in.

The strings that you put together are easy, and you can try it out by creating a ch5.py file that you are going to put all of this information into. The chances are that you will be able to use them for some type of data later, on but do not worry about making them match up with the other sets of data that you have in other files. They will not be used in combination with those and are actually out of order with the rest of the book and the way that the chapters are put together.

Dictionaries

The only other data set that you need to be aware of as a beginner is dictionaries. They are able to help you define exactly what you want when it comes to the various lists that you have. They are the map and the key that your Python will need to decode all of the different things that you are doing. If you are going to have a working program, you will absolutely need to have dictionaries included in with it so that you can try new things and make the most out of what you are using.

The dictionary, when it comes to the grade example that was used earlier in this chapter will help you to figure out what the different things are. We will use initials for the people who got the grades:

assignment1grades= {"JD" : 32, "PG" : 58 "CB" : 12 "MS" : 100}

These are all the grades of the "students" who are being identified by their initials.

When someone goes into the program, they can see that there are different things that people do, and they will be able to see the grades of each of the people depending on what they scored on the tests. For example, you may want to see what JD's grade is. For that, you will create a screen that says:

userIN =raw_input("Whose grade do you want to see?/n")

Then, the person will be able to see what they can do by putting in the initials. There is a chance, though, that they could put the wrong initials in or they could put in someone's name instead of their initial. This will mean that you will have to have something there in case they do:

if userin in assignment1Grades: # different name

print assignment1grades[userin]

else:

print "We don't have that name."

This string shows you that you will be able to tell if they put in the right initials or if they put in something that was totally wrong. If they do put in information that is wrong or they cannot let anyone know about the information that they have, it will be like an error message but just kindly reminding them that it wasn't a valid initial that they put into the input box.

If you are going to use this for anything, you need to make sure that you have that option available to your users. The dictionaries are great, but they will not do anything to make it easier on you when you want to be able to try new things. It is imperative that you try and make sure that all of the information you put into the codes is used for different purposes. Since you are allowing raw input, you won't be able to keep track of every single thing that people are putting into the input boxes, so you have to be prepared for major variables in the way that things are put in.

That's all there is to data sets... not too bad, right?

Chapter 6:

Looping Your Program

When you are creating a program, you will need to make sure that you are able to loop it. Because of the different things that you need to do with the programs that you have, loops are a great way to ensure that you are truly getting the best job possible with the program and while using Python. The loops are great to use for different purposes, and each one has its own specific job when it comes to programming. By making sure that you know all of the different parts of the loops, you can give yourself the best chance possible at success.

Looping While

If a condition that you have set up is true, the while loop is going to remain steady and will keep doing the same thing over and over. You need to make sure that you are using the while loops in the best way possible and that you are going to be able to truly get the most out of the loops so that you can try new things and that you will be able to get what you need out of it.

With game loops, you can use a Boolean that shows the different parts of the loops that you are going to use. It will look something like this:

If userIn.isdigit():

As you learn more about the loop, you can then add in more *while* statements that will help you to identify the different factors that are included with the loops. They will then be able to look something like this if you know what you are doing and add them in the correct way:

total += int(userIn)

This is how you add the integer, and it will change the appearance that comes along with the different aspects of lops. If you are working to create as many loops as possible, you will then need to add new information to it and create different statements that will help you have a more functionable experience with your programming. The next step is to make sure that your loops look like this:

```
else:
print "\nGoodbye!\n" # a goodbye message -- we aren't monsters
run = False
```

After you have put all of the other information into it and you have created the exact type of *while* loop that you want, you'll need to make sure that you can do things like this string of text:

```
run = True
total = 0


while run:
    userIn = raw_input("\n\n\nCurrent total is: %d.\nEnter a number, or anything else to exit.\n" % total)

    if userIn.isdigit():
        total += int(userIn)
    else:
        print "\nGoodbye!\n!"
```

If the object remains the same and is always true each time that it enters into the loop, the loop will continue to spit out the same things. It will also make it easier for you to see the different aspects of the loops that you have.

Your total output will then look like this:

Current total is: 0.
Enter a number, or anything else to exit.
3

Current total is: 3.
Enter a number, or anything else to exit.
9

Current total is: 12.
Enter a number, or anything else to exit.
fl

Goodbye!

When you see this message, you will know that you have reached the point where you have successfully created a *while* loop and that the same thing will consistently show up each time there is a definitive truth to the way that things are done in the programming language that you are using. It is something that you will be able to do and you will be able to make sure of while you are doing different things with your programming.

Looping For

When it comes to Python, *for* loops are different than what they could have been because of the way that they are used and the way that they are set up. It is important that you try to make sure that the *for* loop is something that you are doing in all instances and that you are using it to make sure that things are true about the different avenues you are working on.

The idea behind this type of loop is that it shows the type of data and the sets of data that you are using for your various looping process.

No matter what type of loop you are using or the variable that you are changing with the loops, the "i" identifier will always be something that will go along with it and will help people to be able to see what you are doing.

The idea behind the *for* loop is so that you don't have to write your code out line by line. Instead, you can just write it in a *for* loop and then you'll be able to see the major differences in the loops and what they mean for the different codes that are put into the process.

One of the best parts about using a *for* loop is that you don't always have to have the data sets that are included with your loop.

If you have an open range of data that you plan to use with the loops that you have set up, all you need to do is put a code in that looks like this:

```
for i in range(10):
    print i+1    # i+1 because the computer starts counting at 0
```

The idea of this is because you will not have to worry about data sets. If someone puts something into the loop input generator, you don't need to worry about whether or not it is going to fit into a data set. This is an especially good idea if you are going to use raw inputs or other types of inputs that will have a profound effect on the output that is released from the print command option on your program.

If you want to make sure that you are getting the best option possible for your programming and with the various input categories you have, you will need to make sure that you are using your input amounts and that the loops are going to include everything that you want to have on them.

For loops, while they seem relatively simple, can be especially tricky thanks to the fact that you cannot really determine whether they are going to go through or cause a null statement to come up with the input data. You will need to try your code out, at least, one time before you finalize it to make sure that the *for* statement was created correctly.

Chapter 7:

Python's Methods

There is a lot of stuff that you can do while you are using Python. The majority of things that you do will actually be very complicated and not at all like the simple strings that you have put together throughout the chapters of this book. Be aware that they will be somewhat complicated and that you will need to work with different things to be able to get each of the strings done.

With functions, you would generally need to copy and paste every single line of information that you have into the file that you want to be able to show to people. Methods eliminate this problem and allow you the chance to be able to put the codes to good use instead of spending a long time trying to get it to all fit in.

The actual term method refers to the following:

returndata type with a functionName in it you will then need to put retrun value (not all functions need this part of the code though)

You can do this to create a function depending on the numbers that you want to be able to use:

multiplyNum(number){return number* ; }

You can also create this to get the number input that you want to go into that multiplication sequence:

main {x = multiplyNum (6); }

The function that goes into the equation is the $f(x)$ which is similar to many different things that you may have seen in various math classes throughout your life – further proving that programming and the idea behind Python all goes back to math and what math is able to do in a sense of computing. It all relates back to what you can do with different math equations.

Since you are using Python though, you can easily understand the way that methods work. They are nearly identical to the options that you have with different codes, but Python has made it much easier for you to understand the information that is included with each of these options.

To define a function in Python, all you have to do is let Python know that you are creating a method (which is the exact same thing as a function):

```
def functionName(arguments):
```

```
# code here
```

The next step of functions is to start working with functions on your own. Create your Chapter 7 file by saving it as ch7.py.

After you have created the file, you are going to use it to make a size calculator for your home. It will allow you to put the square footage of the home in, and it will give you an idea of the size of your hypothetical home. You are going to have completely perfectly square rooms in your "home" for the purpose of this file:

```
rooms = []
```

Now, you will need to create the method that is necessary for figuring out what the area of the home is going to be:

```
def calculateArea(length, width):
```

```
print"/nRoom square footage: %d" % (length * width)
```

```
return length * width
```

The function for the room will be as follows:

```
def addRooms(roomlist):
```

```
sqareft: 0
```

The next step is using iteration (do you see where this is going? You're applying all of the principles that you have learned throughout the previous chapters to this function creation). Make your iteration:

for room in roomlist

Now, you can put in the total square footage of the room that you are using:

sqareft + = room # sqareft + room

return sqareft

Now, you will need to know how many rooms are in the house. This is something that you need to do so make sure that you are converting it from a function into an integer so that you can make the new information present for it. There are many different options for doing this, but all you need to do is go back to what you learned in the previous chapters:

int(raw_input) "Number of rooms in house?"))

This is the way that it will be able to change when someone puts some type of input into the room or the house that they have seen in the different areas. It is going to change the number instantly from a string and a part of a list to an integer. From there, it will allow you to see the square footage. Declare the loop you are going to use:

for i in range (romm Count):

Then, get the length and the width of the room that you are going to get

L = int (raw input "How long is the room?")

W = int (raw in put "How wide is the room?")

Now you can get the area by multiplying them and that will tell you the square footage of the room. It will go through the calculator:

area room = calculatearea (length, width)

Then, just add it to the list of the rooms that you have already created

rooms. append (area)

This will allow you to see the total area of the rooms that are in the house. They will be added together in accordance with their individual square footage, and that is the total square footage of the house that you are trying to figure out.

There are so many ways to do this, and you will be able to use your math skills to apply it in a real life situation (like with rooms that are not perfectly square) to be able to find the exact amount. To be able to find rooms that aren't square in the way that these rooms are, all you need to do is subtract the negative space of the rooms from the other square footage of the rooms.

If you want to figure out that type of house, you will need to create a completely different calculator because it will not work at all in the same way as what you would normally be able to do. It is necessary to try and make sure that you are creating the most realistic version of each of the things possible so that when users put their information in, they will get the exact information that they need based on the method that you created.

Chapter 8:

Input and Output of File

The file input and output is necessary if you ever want to do any type of actual programming. You need to use this activity to make sure that you can save your progress, put the data into the fields that they belong, and even be able to pull data out of the information that you have collected. There are so many things that you can do with file I/O that it can sometimes be difficult to figure out what you are doing and the way that it is helping you to work the right way.

Programs like word processors use file input and output because they need to have a way to save the information that you have put into them. If you are saving a file or opening one up, then you are using File I/O and may not even know it because of the way that the program works. Programming the right way makes things like file input and output go almost perfectly and provides nearly seamless integration of the different things that are going on in the situations that you do them.

As with all things related to Python, it is very easy to be able to put the file information and pull the file information when you need it. You don't even have to worry about the problems that most other programs require you to use when you are in different situations. The easiest things that you do with Python will all involve the use of File I/O. It is much easier than any of the other codes that you have written in the past few chapters.

Open

The way that you write files with Python is easy to understand and just as easy to be able to do. You will need to interact with files if you want to be able to try different things so you should make sure that you are doing it in all different areas that you have worked with and will continue to work for you if you make sure that you are doing it the right way.

To open, you will just need to know the interaction modes:

operator meaning description

w write mode – erases the file that you wrote, writes it from scratch

r read mode – allows you to read the file and nothing else

r+ – read the file or write it so that you can position yourself

a – append mode allows you to add content onto the file that you created

Similar to what you experience with certain word processing documents and programs that allow you to process, you will automatically get the read-only outlook if that is what you are looking for. So, if you want a read only document or processing option, then all you need to do is not specify the interaction mode. If you don't do it, it will default. If you want it to be anything other than read-only, you'll need to make sure that you can specify it.

f = open

Create ch8.py.

Write the code to open the file with example.txt. This will allow you to open something that is in write-only mode. You do not have to worry about what you are erasing because there is nothing on the actual file that will ever be erased since nothing was on the file in the beginning. This is how your code should look:

f = open ("example.txt", "w")

You'll need to add a loop to this so that you can try new things with the options that come up. You won't have to worry about the different things that are associated with the text if you open it in a loop and if you work to make sure that they are *truly* looping through the different documents. This is what your string will look like with the loop:

for i in range(9)

f. write ("%d/n*% (i + 1))

The total amount of it is going to show up when the file opens. This will happen each time there is a user who puts the information in and when there is a change to the way that the information is processed. If you want to be done with the file, you will need to close it.

Close

Similar to opening a file like you did in Python, closing is simple. The only thing that you need to write down in the code to close up the file and to allow things to go back to the way that they were is as follows:

f.close()

If you are going to have a document and you are going to be able to process it while using the program that you created, you will need to have a string of text. This is the code, and it can be put into the program so that you will be able to make changes to it whenever you want. While it seemed like each of the steps were really simple, they all led up to this:

f = open (example. txt" , "w")

for i in range (9):

f. write ("%D/n*%(i+1))

f. close

Save all of the information that you wrote down in your plain text to make sure that it is under the ch8.py file and that it is able to be run on your program. Open up Python (if it isn't already open) and run it.

This should allow you to see the document that you created.

Since you were using the integer way of doing it and you chose to have the range stop at 9, you would be able to make sure that you are seeing all of the numbers that are 1 through 9. Since you are not using the function and, instead, used integers, you will not be able to see 0 as it is not an integer.

Chapter 9:

The Basics of OOP

When programming first became a popular option for people who previously worked in the technology sector, the codes that were written were, essentially, written in stone because of the way that they were used and because the code had to run the entire course before any changes could be made. Even then, changes were often not able to make a difference with the way that things were going and the way that the codes were written.

Now, though, you can easily make changes to the way that a program runs and operates. This is something that will allow you the chance to be able to see that there are major differences in each of the programs and the way that they are run. It is a good idea to try new things, but to be able to do that, you will need to know more about OOP.

OOP is the acronym for object-oriented programming. There was a language in the past that was called Ada, and it was used to make the OOP. This was something that was huge for the programming industry, and it was able to change the way that people would do programming forever. When someone created a code, they could now use that code to be able to make changes later on. They were not limited to the first time that they made a code, and they no longer had to worry about the problems that would come from using the different options that were included with codes. Thanks to Ada and OOP, programming is now much easier, and you can make major changes any time that you want to make them.

The idea behind OOP is that it has both classes and objects that are present in it. What was originally Ada developed into what is now known as Java, and it was able to grow from that point. Because of the changes that were made to the programming industry during that time, OOP became the norm and became something that people would be able to do no matter what they wanted to add into their programming field. It allowed them the chance to be able to try new things and to get what they could out of the different aspects of programming.

Below, we'll take a closer look at the classes and objects that make up OOP. In Chapter 10, you'll learn more about the specifics of OOP and how it can be used with your programming, which is the last true step to take you from a complete beginner to someone who knows how to do programming with Python. OOP is basically made up of the following:

Classes – These are concepts that change the characteristics of a program. They are the specific little details that can change what you are doing with your programming and with the different things that you have. In the next chapter, you will learn about cars as a class. This is something that is usually somewhat difficult to learn but is also something that will allow you the chance to see what you can do to make changes. Every car has wheels, a motor, and something that you can steer with, but not all of them are exactly the same. Think of your data as the car and then the other pieces of the car as the pieces that make up the data. That is the easiest way for you to understand a class and how it relates to OOP.

Objects – This is the instance of the class that you already created. While the class defines the data as a whole, the object defines exactly what the object is. For example, an object can be the difference between a big car and a little car, or it could be the difference between your car and my car. There are many major differences that come along with the objects and what that means for the objects, so make sure that you are using that to your advantage and that you are doing what you can to figure out the instances that come along with the classes that you have.

When you are able to see the way that you can declare a class by using Python, you can have a better sense of the way that they work. When you are just thinking of classes in terms of cars and colors and whose is what, it can be harder to understand the way that it works and what it does with the different options. If you are creating a class in Python, it will allow you to see the way that it works out by giving you the information like this:

class className(parent class):
definitive _ iniit ___ ():
relevant variables that go into the class.
If you are going to use the example like we were using, it would be written out like this:
definitiveCar(object):
After that, you can make sure that you are using the different terms that can be adjusted in the classes and with the options that you will need in your instances. As you learn more about vehicle classes and the options

that are included with them, you can see the different ways that the class works and the way that they are able to be used to your own advantage within the class options. If you use a class to define an object, you will need to make sure that you use variables as the objects:

definitive_ init_ (self, make Model, Year, wheel)

You will then need to try to define each of the classes by using:

self.makemodel = make and model

self year = year producted

self wheels = number of wheels

You can add each of these things, and it will allow you the chance to see that you are going to define the specifics that come along with different vehicle classes and the way that they work to make them a part of the coding that you are doing.

Chapter 10:

How to Use OOP

Now that you know what OOP is and how it works in accordance with your Python programming, it is important that you look at all of the concepts that come along with OOP and the way that they can be used.

In this chapter, you can expect to learn more about the way that OOP works and the way that you can make sure that you are using different options for your python experience. It will give you a chance to try new things and to add different elements to the programming that you created. It is also something that will give you the ability to make major changes to the way that things are done in your Python experience. Your programs will give you the chance to see how you can make the coding process easier and how you can include various options with the codes that you write.

Inherit

The "inheritance" factor is one of the concepts that you will learn when you are using OOP. It is the simplest and most widely used concept that you can write with on Python. It also gives you the chance to learn new things about the programs that you are writing and gives you the ability to make major changes with the experience that you have on Python.

By looking at vehicles again, you can have a better understanding of how inheritance works.

All SUVS are vehicles. Not all of the vehicles that are available are going to be SUVS though. All vans are vehicles, and again, not all vehicles are vans. When you are looking at the different types of vehicles, you can clearly see that not all vans are SUVS and there are actually a lot more vehicles than just those two that you can use for different things.

The concept behind OOP is that things can be broken down into the smallest part possible, like this:

Vehicles -> SUVS -> Four Wheel Drive -> Class (seating) -> Make -> Model -> Trim

By looking at this, you can see that the vehicle is the actual parent that is used in the situation while the Trim becomes the child for it. There can only be one parent for a certain set of classifications, but there can be many children that the parent has.

If you were going to use the same sequence to be able to convert the information into your own Python codes and then be able to put the information out on your site or wherever you are using your programming for, it would look like this:

```
class Vehicle(object):
    def __init__(self, makeAndModel, prodYear, airConditioning):
        self.makeAndModel = makeAndModel
        self.prodYear = prodYear
        self.airConditioning = airConditioning
        self.doors = 4


    def honk(self):
        print "%s says: Honk! Honk!" % self.makeAndModel
```

To make sure that you would have everything that you need in the code, you would actually need to write it:

```
class SportsCar(Vehicle)
    def __init__(self, makeAndModel, prodYear, airConditioning):
    self.makeAndModel = makeAndModel
    self.prodYear = prodYear
    self.airConditioning = airConditioning
    self.doors = 4
```

By doing this, you will give yourself the chance to see that there are many different options that can go into the codes, and that will give you the chance to see the different aspects of each of the codes that you have. You will need to make sure that you are doing what you can with the codes you are working with so that you will be able to do more with it and so that you can include everything that is necessary in the codes that you are using with your Python.

You can test it all out and use the exact code that is included there to be able to bring it up on the program that you have created with Python.

Polymorph

With the same idea behind inheritance, polymorphism allows for the changes to be made to the different aspects that are included with the fares on all of the different changes that you are making. When you are able to use polymorphism, you will make sure that you are getting the best experience possible and that you can make some changes without ever having to go into the code. If you are going to use it for Python, you will need to use method overloading or overriding.

When you are able to use overloading to change the way that coding appears, you will need to write it so that there is a lot of code in one area. This will "overload" the system and will cause it to stop with the changes that you want to make. There will be too much for it to process, and this is something that can completely change the system. Either it will not pick up on the information that you have put into the code, or it will cause it to become completely deleted within the way that it is done.

If you are going to use overriding, you will need to write a code that is capable of overriding the entire system. Just because you need to get rid of once instance of the code does not mean that you will be able to choose the area that you want to get deleted. It is important that you try to make sure that you are using what you can to be able to make those changes and that each of the changes that you make will depend on the entire system. After you have overridden the system, you need to add additional information to it and put it into play so that you can change the way it functions.

Now that you are aware of all of the changes that you can make after you have written your code, you will be able to make the changes that you want. It won't necessarily mean that you are going to have those changes, but it will give you a chance to try more and to do more with the areas that you are using.

You should feel less pressure when putting your code together and trying the different files out since you now know that it is all able to be fixed through either polymorphism or inheritance.

Chapter 11:

How to Use Your Python Skills

There are many ways that you can use the skills that you have just learned to be able to try Python and use it for yourself. Once you know how to use Python, you can do all of your own programming, and that will give you the help that you need to be able to get started with your career in programming. Gone are the days where you need to rely on programs that are created by other people or the "expert" help of people who really can't do much to help you. After reading this book, you will be more than just a beginner, and you will be able to use that to your benefit so that you can do everything from providing yourself with a service to making a lucrative income.

Power a Social Media Site

You may be surprised to find out that those Instas you loved earlier today are possible because of Python. With the capabilities that Python has, you can not only build an entire social media site but also power it.

While many of the other social media sites have moved onto "bigger" languages that are just a few steps up from Python, Instagram still uses Python to power everything that they do. You will be able to do the same, and hopefully, one day have a social media site that is just as famous as Instagram.

Create a Fun Game for Friends

Throughout this book, you learned the way to make different things and give people choices for what they were going to put into your input areas. These are all choices that they can make, but you can benefit by putting them into a game. Whether you want to be a game creator or not is irrelevant. Building a game for your friends to play online (or off!) is a great way to practice your Python skills and have a better chance at building really cool stuff in the future.

In the beginning, you can start with a very basic game. Users are asked input questions, and the output is all based on that information. The better you get at writing Python, the more advanced your games can be. You may even be able to make something that is comparable to your favorite video game. From there, take your skills to a different place and you'll be a true Python master in no time!

Learn Insider Secrets

There are no *real* secrets of Python, but as you begin to work with more codes and try new things out, you will be able to learn some of the quirks that the language comes with so that you can try new things and you'll be able to find out some of the things that the most advanced Python users have. This is a great way to learn new things, try out new codes, and give yourself a chance at doing more with the Python language so that you can take it to the next level.

You can also use Python if you want to enter any program through the back door. While it isn't necessarily the best hacking language that is available for you to try, it is something that you can get very comfortable with getting the specifics on other programs with. It will give you a chance to do much more than simply creating websites, programs, or other things that can sometimes be complicated for you to figure out.

The Language of Google

The language that Google uses is the same language that you are beginning to learn all about. Google is one of the biggest sites on the Internet and possibly the most-visited around the world depending on which statistics you look at. If something as big as Google continues to use Python, then it is a relatively good language to learn.

One thing that you can do is teach yourself how the programming and the codes of Google work. While I wouldn't necessarily suggest trying to compete with Google, you can try to learn more so that you will be able to give yourself a better chance with the options that you have. One of those options would be to try and get a job with Google. Having Python knowledge will help you get a job at nearly any tech-related industry.

Build on Your Knowledge

For many people who just want to know the basics, Python is the end of the line. For others, though, it can be a simple stepping stone to learning more coding language. The majority of people who know the more complicated methods of writing in different code languages started with Python and continue to use it while they are working on different languages.

One of the best parts of being able to use Python to build on the knowledge that you have is that you will always be able to learn more from what you are doing and what you have done with Python. None of the languages that are present in today's world are exactly the same, but knowing one code language will often help you to have a better chance at learning a different one.

Make Money

Aside from the already mentioned idea of getting a job with Google or some other industry leader that uses Google, you can make your own money by yourself. You don't need another company to be able to show you what to do. This is something that you can do once you master Python and something that is going to be very lucrative depending on how you market yourself.

The next chapter will give you all of the ideas that you need to truly make Python your career. No more begging for jobs and trying to get big-name companies to hire you with your limited knowledge of Python that, while impressive to you, pales in comparison to some of the biggest programmers who work with those companies.

Chapter 12:

How to Make Money with Python

Once you have learned Python and the way to make sure that you are creating the perfect program, you will be able to start making money with it. Some people may be tempted to go to companies or businesses and ask them to hire them, but that is not where the real money is. If you want to truly make money with Python, you need to go your own way and make sure that you are doing it right.

Follow these steps to launch your Python career and earn yourself some financial freedom:

Practice

You will absolutely need to practice with Python. You should not try to go out on your own and start a career after reading this book. Read it again. Try new things on Python. Use variations. Look for new codes. All of these will help you to practice and will give you a chance to see which aspects of Python you are good at and which ones could stand to have a little more practice.

Remember, though, that you will get better if you practice a lot.

Create

It is necessary to create things with Python for yourself before you are able to create them for other people. Since you have a skill, you will need to use it for your own good first. Try to make some games, design a program, and prepare yourself to do more for other people. Think of things that people may want you to create for them and do them for yourself. This will allow you to keep practicing but will also put your knowledge to work so that you can use it later on when you are listing the work that you did.

List

Create a list of all of the things that you have done with Python. Build a site using Python and make sure that you connect it with the things that you have done. Give yourself a killer domain name and then design the site so that it is seamless. This is your portfolio. It is where you will direct people to when you are talking about your services. It is also where your work will be showcased, so be sure to always show off your best Python programming.

Advertise

Advertising yourself is as simple as advertising a business. Let them know that they need you, not the other way around. If you offer a service that they need and that they can't refuse, you'll be able to advertise yourself much more easily. It is a good idea to try and make sure that you are doing what you can to advertise yourself in a positive light. Use social media, networking opportunities, and even chances offline to advertise the fact that you are able to do programming. Always remember to include the link to your portfolio so that they can see the work that you have done.

Prove Value

Some people may balk at the prices that you are charging them especially if they have never tried to hire a programmer before. Make sure that you show them why it costs so much to hire you. They will be much easier to retain if you can prove that you are valuable.

Negotiate

The chances are that you are going to have to negotiate especially when you are first getting started with your Python programming career. There is nothing wrong with this even if you think that you are worth more than what someone wants to pay you for the work that you are doing. Keep all of this in mind when you start to forget why you were doing it in the first place. The negotiation process can be tricky, but you'll be able to do the most if you do negotiate in the beginning.

Collect

Sit back and collect on the money that you can make from programming. You stand to have a very lucrative career if you make sure that you always do the best work possible, you provide people with a reason to want to hire you, and you show them that you are extremely valuable when it comes to the services that you offer. Are you ready for financial freedom thanks to Python?

Conclusion

Thank for making it through to the end of *Python: A Complete Step-by-Step Beginners Guide to Programming with Python*. Let's hope it was informative and able to provide you with all of the tools you need to achieve your goals.

The next step is to download Python and make sure that you are using it to go through each chapter of this book. If you didn't in the beginning, go back and download it so that you can get the most out of the book.

Finally, if you found this book useful in any way, a review on Amazon is always appreciated!

The information in the following pages is broadly considered to be a truthful and accurate account of facts, and as such any inattention, use or misuse of the information in question by the reader will render any resulting actions solely under their purview. There are no scenarios in which the publisher or the original author of this work can be in any fashion deemed liable for any hardship or damages that may befall them after undertaking information described herein.

Additionally, the information found on the following pages is intended for informational purposes only and should thus be considered, universal. As befitting its nature, the information presented is without assurance regarding its continued validity or interim quality. Trademarks that mentioned are done without written consent and can in no way be considered an endorsement from the trademark holder.

84826041R00102

Made in the USA
Columbia, SC
19 December 2017